Amos Kamau

Market entry strategy

GRIN Verlag

Bibliografische Information der Deutschen Nationalbibliothek:

Die Deutsche Bibliothek verzeichnet diese Publikation in der Deutschen National-
bibliografie; detaillierte bibliografische Daten sind im Internet über http://dnb.d-
nb.de/ abrufbar.

Dieses Werk sowie alle darin enthaltenen einzelnen Beiträge und Abbildungen
sind urheberrechtlich geschützt. Jede Verwertung, die nicht ausdrücklich vom
Urheberrechtsschutz zugelassen ist, bedarf der vorherigen Zustimmung des Verla-
ges. Das gilt insbesondere für Vervielfältigungen, Bearbeitungen, Übersetzungen,
Mikroverfilmungen, Auswertungen durch Datenbanken und für die Einspeicherung
und Verarbeitung in elektronische Systeme. Alle Rechte, auch die des auszugsweisen
Nachdrucks, der fotomechanischen Wiedergabe (einschließlich Mikrokopie) sowie
der Auswertung durch Datenbanken oder ähnliche Einrichtungen, vorbehalten.

Imprint:

Copyright © 2011 GRIN Verlag GmbH
Druck und Bindung: Books on Demand GmbH, Norderstedt Germany
ISBN: 978-3-656-57520-7

This book at GRIN:

http://www.grin.com/en/e-book/265519/market-entry-strategy

GRIN - Your knowledge has value

Der GRIN Verlag publiziert seit 1998 wissenschaftliche Arbeiten von Studenten, Hochschullehrern und anderen Akademikern als eBook und gedrucktes Buch. Die Verlagswebsite www.grin.com ist die ideale Plattform zur Veröffentlichung von Hausarbeiten, Abschlussarbeiten, wissenschaftlichen Aufsätzen, Dissertationen und Fachbüchern.

Visit us on the internet:

http://www.grin.com/

http://www.facebook.com/grincom

http://www.twitter.com/grin_com

Introduction

Different market entry strategies can be used to enter a new market, these strategies include mergers, acquisitions, joint ventures, exporting, Greenfield project, strategic alliances, franchising/licensing and whole subsidiary ownership (Janssen 2004, p. 556). Some of the factors that influence the choice of a market entry strategy include price localization, trade barriers, competition, export subsidies and localized knowledge (Grunig & Morschett 2012, p. 151). Globalization and foreign direct investments have been vital in global expansion of companies (Hill 2005, p. 67). This study suggests licensing as a market entry strategy that could be adopted by Rodl & Partner in its entry to South Africa (Rodl & Partner, 2012). South Africa is one of the well known markets that have well developed accounting, auditing and consulting industry and this makes the selection a suitable one for Rodl & Partner. South Africa enjoys a stable and developing economy and this has been a key attraction for foreign investors.

Rodl & Partner Ltd

Background of the company

Rodl & Partner is an international consulting and accounting firm with German origin. The company has established and built unique capabilities in the global consulting industry particularly in accounting, tax planning and attestation services for companies across various continents. The company has about 3200 partners located in about 130 countries across globe. The company provides customers with distinctive and high quality service in the various categories of accounting services (Rodl & Partner, 2012). Rodl & Partner has its strengths in tax, assurance and specialist advice. Rodl & Partner will be entering South African accounting and consulting industry in July 2012 and this will require the company to be well prepared in expanding its business in this new market so as to be able to promote its brand awareness in the global market.

PESTEL analysis

Economic environment: South Africa has risen from international isolation and economic stagnation caused by apartheid era. The new phase of economic reconstruction has received encouragement and acclaim internationally (Thompson 2001, p. 23). The country was rated 25th in terms of advanced industrial sectors in the world in 1990s and has since then marked increasing growth.

Political and legal environment: South Africa has had stability in its political and legal systems. Policies made by government are focused on strengthening economic power of the country and this makes the political environment welcoming for investors (Thompson 2001, p. 44). Since 1994, South Africa's legislation has focused on compensating about 3.5 million of citizens who faced displacement during apartheid and this has been vital in reducing crime in the country and making the economy open for foreign investment.

Technology environment: the economy has been characterized by rapid expansion and growth as domestic and foreign investors invest in technological developments in the various industries (Thompson 2001, p. 32).

Social and cultural environments: South Africa has approximately 50 million people. The culture of South Africa is diverse. The country comprise of both blacks and the whites. The country is increasingly urbanized with about 8 different languages in use (Thompson 2001, p. 14). The most common language is English though other languages including Khoisan language and Hindi among others exist.

Physical environment: the country has temperate climate since it is surrounded by Indian and Atlantic Ocean (Thompson 2001, p. 69). The country is known as a global biodiversity hotspot with different species of flora and fauna and this has greatly promoted the tourism industry as well as many other economic sectors.

South Africa's accounting industry

Analysis using Porter's five forces

Competitive rivalry: Competitive rivalry in the accounting and consulting business is often high since firms differentiate their services into various combinations such as human resource, corporate finance, technology development and consultancy, operations management and business process outsourcing among others (Black Enterprise 1999, p. 89). South Africa's accounting and consulting industry is a highly competitive industry whose competitive rivalry is high. There are many firms both small and large audit firs that are established in South Africa. In addition, firms like Earnest and Young, Price Water Coopers and several other well known global auditing brands have their presence in the market. This makes competitive in the industry stiff and challenges the new firms entering the market.

2

Threat of new entrants: the capital is not capital intensive and this makes new entrants the a real threat in the industry. New establishments in the industry require very highly professionalized partners to be able to compete with the existing partners from other market players. Rodl & Partner establishment in South Africa would face competitors like PWC, Earnst & Young, KPMG among others and must therefore design its entry strategy well in order to be able to sustain its business in the market.

New substitutes' threats: In terms of threat of substitutes, the alternative to accounting and consulting services include in-house support and planning in firms that focus on reducing the cost on consulting. This implies that value addition and differentiation of services will be integral to the services offered by Rodl & Partner. The accounting and consulting industry requires little capital to start, it is not capital intensive and this makes it easy for new firms to enter the market. However, consulting requires substantial intellectual and human labor, which can be developed over time.

Suppliers' bargaining power: Credibility and reputation of the partners is integral to a firm's success and this makes it possible for only a few firms to compete though the industry has several entrants. There few well rounded consultants and this makes suppliers bargaining power a little high.

Buyers' bargaining power: Companies have continued to increase their in-house development of consulting teams making and this reduces the willing buyers of the consulting services from consulting firms. In general, the market bargaining power though high may become relatively low if the trend by companies continues.

SWOT Analysis

Strengths: Rodl & Partner offers clients benefits of knowledgeable audit partners and great experience in the industry. The company has built a strong reputation for its financial due diligence in law, taxation, finance and other aspects of its business (Rodl & Partner, 2012). This provides a strong and competitive brand for South Africa's accounting and consulting market. It also promotes confidence of the clients in the company's services.

Weaknesses: Rodl & Partner has concentrated mainly in Europe and United States and has not invested much in Africa. The company has not yet known the African market well.

Opportunities: South Africa's accounting industry is well known for expertise and skills that are built by the consulting firms. For this reason, small firms often approach the large audit firms to access skills and build knowledge on auditing. This is an attractive aspect of the market particularly for companies seeking entry in the market since they are assured of available skilled labor and expertise. The recent football hosting of the World Cup 2010 has made the country more attractive to foreign service providers Cape Town has become an attractive region for social and economic growth in the globe (Rodl & Partner, 2012).

Threat: South Africa's accounting industry is faced with uncertainties as well as imminent changes following the implementation of a new companies' act. The small auditing firms are challenged to join the huge auditing firms in order to retain their auditing exposure (Centre on Transnational Corporations 2008, p. 51). The auditing firms are required to have in place IFRS advisor and a reporting accountant. They are also required to have an audit partner who is trained in three courses spelt out by the JSE as headline earnings per share, Reporting accountant specialist training and auditors' general requirements for listing.

Market entry strategy

Licensing

From the analysis done on the industry, South Africa is one of the promising consulting markets. The best entry strategy for Rodl & Partner into the new market would therefore be licensing of a local partner already in the market. Rodl & Partner Ltd will approach one of the auditing and consulting companies in South Africa and request for licensing to trade under its brand name in the local market. The only thing required of the firm will be to start trading with the well known global brand. Since Rodl & Partner has a well established reputation across the Global consulting industry, the company will not struggle to get the licensing bids from the local South Africa's consulting industry. Licensing is mostly applied in the consulting and the technological industry. Licensing involves establishing strategic alliance through sale of intellectual property of right to use specified proprietary knowledge in a defined way (Gillespie et al 2008, p. 256).

Advantages of licensing strategy

The party licensing does not incur development risks and costs, licensing is thus attractive for those firms that may not have adequate capital or may not be willing to invest a lot of capital (Doole & Lowe 2008, p. 387). Rodl & Partner will not incur costs like the purchasing or leasing of business premises, establishment of new customers, human capital and many other costs or risks (Hitt et al 2010, p. 232). Rodl & Partner will avoid the costly and stringent compliance and legal requirements that are in place in South Africa as required by the country's companies' act. Another advantage of use of international licensing as an entry strategy in markets where there are constraints, barriers of entry since the strategy enables a firm to enter the new market where foreigners are prohibited (John & Letto 1996, p. 267). Licensing enables the licensor to make business relationships with potential industry partners in the market (Doole & Lowe 2008, p. 389).

Disadvantages of licensing as an entry method

One of challenges with this strategy is that it does not give the licensor control over business activities and processes, business strategy and other important aspects of the company. This is because the licensor takes no part in setting up of the operations and this can severely limit the licensor from identifying inefficiencies (Gillespie et al 2008, p. 257). Licensing also places limitation on the licensors ability to use the profits earned from one market to support the company's business in another market, which is sometimes necessary in overcoming competitive attacks. The licensor is only allowed to use its royalty payments to fund other licensees operating in other markets with the brand. Licensing also puts the licensor at the risk of losing its technological know-how to the licensee. Licensing can be used by licensee to actually position himself as the future market leader over the licensor (Gillespie et al 2008, p. 257).

Conclusion

This study has identified Rodl & Partner one of the German's accounting and consulting firms and explored the most appropriate strategy for the company when entering South Africa's accounting and consulting market. South Africa has a well built consulting industry and the industry is highly competitive particularly for small auditing firms that so often are forced to join the big auditing firms to improve their experience and realize their viability. For the competitive South Africa's industry, licensing strategy has been identified as the most appropriate market entry strategy wing to the various benefits such as fewer risks and costs, ease of implementations and many others (Drabner 2008, p. 18).

Rodl & Partner should adopt a licensing strategy to enter South Africa's accounting market. The company should ensure that it has studied the local market well and that it has understood the legal requirements and compliance needs for the new market. Such knowledge would be crucial in understanding whether the company selected for licensing is in compliance with the countries law as stipulated in the companies' act of the country. The licensing agreements should spell out terms and conditions of the licensing contract to avoid unnecessary cancellations. Rodl & Partner should select its licensee carefully to avoid trading its know-how against the plan and desire of the firm. One way to avoid such unintended transfers would be by establishing cross-licensing agreements, which involves requesting the licensee to also give its valuable know-how in addition to the royalty payments (Bilewicz 2007, p. 16).

References

Bilewicz, E (2007), *The Optimization of Market Entry Strategies Focused on Market Entry Barriers*...Munich, GRIN Verlag.

Black Enterprise (1999), *Business consultants*, Dallas, Black Enterprise

Centre on Transnational Corporations (United Nations) (2008), *International accounting and reporting issues,* Washington, D.C. United Nations Publications

Doole, I & Lowe, R (2008), *International marketing strategy: analysis, development and implementation*, London, CengageBrain.com.

Drabner, T (2008), *Market entry strategies and their applicability to SMEs- The winding road to...* Munich, GRIN Verlag.

Gillespie, K, Jeanet, J & Hennessey, D (2008), *Global Marketing*, London, CengageBrain.com.

Rodl & Partner (2012), website link:
http://www.roedl.com/locations/americas/united_states_of_america.html

Grunig, R & Morschett, D (2012), *Developing International Strategies: Going and Being International for ...*New York, Springer.

Hill, C (2005), *International business with Global Resource CD, PowerWeb and World Map* (5th Ed.).New York: McGraw Hill

Hitt, M, Ireland, D & Hoskisson, R (2010), *Strategic Management: Competitiveness & Globalization, Concepts,* London, CengageBrain.com.

Janssen, M (2004), On durable goods markets with entry and adverse selection, *Canadian Journal of Economics*, Vol. 37(3), pp. 552-589

John, R & Letto, G (1996), *Global Business Strategy*, London, CengageBrain.com.

Root, F (1994), *Entry strategies for international markets*, Lexington Books, Lexington, MA.

Thompson, L (2001), *A History of South Africa, Third Edition,* London, Yale University Press.